THE SELF-MANAGING COMPANY

Text **60 Minutes**	The length of our small books is based on the time in the air of a flight between Toronto and Chicago. Start reading as you take off and finish the book by the time you land. Just the right length for the 21st-century reader.
Cartoons **30 Minutes**	You can also ⬚⬚⬚⬚⬚⬚⬚⬚⬚⬚⬚ ⬚⬚ ⬚⬚⬚⬚ e ideas in this book ⬚⬚⬚⬚⬚⬚⬚⬚⬚⬚⬚ ⬚⬚⬚ eading the captions. We find the cartoons have made our Strategic Coach concepts accessible to readers as young as eight years old.
Audio **120 Minutes**	The audio recording that accompanies this book is not just a recitation of the printed words, but an in-depth commentary that expands each chapter's mindset into new dimensions. Download the audio at **strategiccoach.com/go/smcebook**
Video **60 Minutes**	Our video synopsis of The Self-Managing Company deepens your understanding of all eight mindsets. If you combine text, cartoons, audio, and video, your understanding of the ideas will be 10x greater than you would gain from reading only. Watch the videos at **strategiccoach.com/go/smcebook**
Scorecard **10 Minutes**	Fold out the back cover of the book to score your own readiness and willingness to create a Self-Managing Company. First, score yourself on where you are now, and then fill in where you want to be a year from now. Download additional copies at **strategiccoach.com/go/smcebook**
ebook **1 Minute**	After absorbing the fundamental ideas that describe a Self-Managing Company, you can quickly and easily share them by sending the ebook version to as many other individuals as you desire. Direct them to **strategiccoach.com/go/smcebook**

Thanks to the Creative Team:

Adam Morrison

Kerri Morrison

Hamish MacDonald

Shannon Waller

Jennifer Bhatthal

Victor Lam

Margaux Yiu

Christine Nishino

Willard Bond

Peggy Lam

The Self-Managing Company

In my Strategic Coach workshops, I'll draw a circle on the white board, and in the center, I'll write, "Self-Managing Company."

I'll say to the group, "You don't know exactly what I'm going to say about this, but right off the bat, how many of you want one of these?" Every hand in the room goes up.

Every ambitious entrepreneur in the world wants to have their own Self-Managing Company.

This 60-minute book will provide you and your Unique Ability Team with the eight crucial entrepreneurial mindsets necessary to make this a daily, exciting breakthrough for the next 25 years and beyond.

Strategic Coach®, The Strategic Coach® Program, Unique Ability®, Unique Ability® Team, Unique Ability® Teamwork, The Self-Managing Company®, The 4 C's Formula®, Free Days™, Focus Days™, Buffer Days™, The Entrepreneurial Time System®, The Largest Cheque®, The 10x Mind Expander®, The Lifetime Extender®, WinStreak®, The Self-Multiplying Company™, The Strategic Coach® Signature Program, and The 10x Ambition Program™ are trademarks of The Strategic Coach Inc.

Cartoons by Hamish MacDonald.

Printed in Toronto, Canada. The Strategic Coach Inc., 33 Fraser Avenue, Suite 201, Toronto, Ontario, M6K 3J9.

This publication is meant to strengthen your common sense, not to substitute for it. It is also not a substitute for the advice of your doctor, lawyer, accountant, or any of your advisors, personal or professional.

If you would like further information about the Strategic Coach® Program or other Strategic Coach® services and products, please telephone 416.531.7399 or 1.800.387.3206.

Library and Archives Canada Cataloguing in Publication

Sullivan, Dan, 1944-, author
     The self-managing company / Dan Sullivan.

ISBN 978-1-897239-48-3 (softcover)

     1. Organization. 2. Management. 3. Personnel management.
4. Industrial relations. I. Title.

HD31.2.S85 2017   658   C2017-901309-2

Contents

Introduction
The company everyone wants.
You transform your company into a self-managing organization that continually frees you up for multiplier breakthroughs.

I've had a recurring experience since I first came up with the idea of The Self-Managing Company. In my workshops, I'll draw a circle on the white board, and in the center, I'll write, "Self-Managing Company." I'll say to the group, "You don't know exactly what I'm going to say about this, but right off the bat, how many of you want one of these?"

Every hand in the room goes up.

Having a company that manages itself to greater growth and success, without the owner having to be involved in all aspects of the day-to-day management of the business, is a universal desire for all entrepreneurs.

You are your most important resource.
I often quote French philosopher Jean-Baptiste Say who, in 1803, defined an entrepreneur as someone who shifts resources from a lower to a higher level of productivity and greater yield. But many entrepreneurs don't realize that in order for their company to be successful, the number-one resource that has to be taken to a higher level of productivity is themselves.

In order to do this, they have to be freed up from all activities to focus only on what they love to do, do best, and brings in the most money to their organization.

Many entrepreneurs have the idea that they should free up everybody else in their company before freeing themselves up. They worry that doing otherwise would seem self-centered or egotistical. But this freedom for your team won't happen without your guidance, example, and permission — because if you're not giving yourself permission to be freed up, there's no possibility of any of your team members being able to free themselves up.

Once you're freed up in this way, you can have a creative, cooperative, growth relationship with your own company.

The two decisions that set you apart.
Before you became an entrepreneur, you made two key decisions. Both involved a willingness to take risks that most other people aren't willing to take. The first decision was that you wouldn't depend on anyone else for your own financial success. The second was that you wouldn't expect any opportunity in the marketplace until you first created value for others.

Trace these two decisions back to the time you made them, and you'll realize that nobody ever asked you to do this. Nobody compelled you to be an entrepreneur. This is strictly something that you wanted.

And having made these decisions, you're potentially free to continually create your own future based on your biggest vision. Only someone who's made these two entrepreneurial decisions can build a Self-Managing Company.

Expanding your entrepreneurial freedoms.
Anyone who makes these decisions and embarks on an entrepreneurial path does so to experience greater freedom. It's this potential for freedom that gives entrepreneurs the

original motivation, courage, and confidence to take the risk of going out on their own.

This entrepreneurial freedom can be broken down into four types: Time—Control over your time and the freedom to devote it, both at work and outside of work, to whatever you choose. Money—There's no upper limit or restriction to how much money you can make. Relationship—You get to work with the people you want to work with, including clients, team members, and vendors. Purpose—The entrepreneurial company you've created is not just for your business career, but a vehicle for increasingly living your life the way you want to live it and achieving the things that are most important to you.

Entrepreneurism requires a company.

To fully realize these four entrepreneurial freedoms, you must own your own company. If you're just self-employed without a team, you're the owner of your business, but you're also the staff, which means that whatever ability gave you the confidence and courage to become an entrepreneur, stick with it, and grow will also reach a point where you can't grow any further.

To grow your company beyond this point, you'll need other people with talents and strengths that are different from and complementary to your own. These team members may work in an office with you or they might be virtual team members you've never met in person. But you can't be freed up if there's no one to free you up.

Persisting in working without a team is an anti-growth mentality. If you don't have a company, you can't have a Self-Managing Company.

Company manages everything predictable.

In any business, there are several ongoing, predictable things happening that can be managed by people other than the entrepreneur.

How the existing cash flow is made, for example, might be a predictable process in your organization that doesn't need to involve you. In Strategic Coach, with 15 coaches for the Signature Program and salespeople to bring clients into those workshops, we can pretty well predict what our cash flow is going to be for the year.

Then there's the innovation side of things, where you're creating new value that generates new cash flow. The prime difference between the existing and the new is that the new is usually much more profitable. It also tends to be easier to do and take less time.

This innovation is possible because you're completely freed up from everything predictable in your organization, leaving you to focus only on what you do best. There are those who feel they need to have an active role in every aspect of their business, but you can't have an innovative, increasingly more profitable company unless you have a Self-Managing Company.

With the day-to-day activities of running your business managed by your team, you're free to look at the big picture vision, continually innovate greater and greater value, and even transform your marketplace.

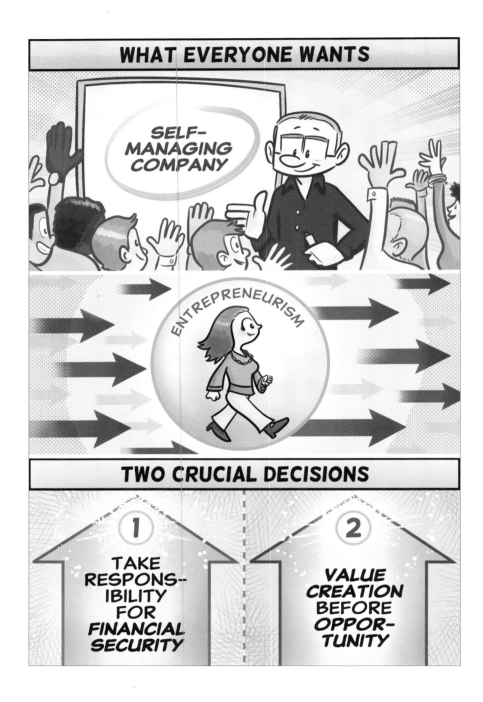

Chapter 1
The ABC Model

You increasingly free yourself to focus more time and attention on breakthroughs that fascinate and motivate you.

As the most important resource in your company, you have to free yourself up to focus your time and attention on breakthroughs that grow your business. The ABC Model that follows is a thinking process you can use every 90 days to shift your focus more and more into areas that you always find exciting, enjoyable, and profitable.

Simplify into three emotional zones.

Those who work in bureaucratic organizations soon learn that it's wise to keep their emotions to themselves or disconnect from them entirely. They're rewarded with greater influence, power, position, status, recognition, and money to the degree that they can depersonalize.

Entrepreneurs are just the opposite. You have to emotionalize every part of your life, and you have to get 100 percent value from your emotional responses to everyday life. Those responses will occur across a spectrum, from very negative to very positive, depending on what activities you personally are involved with.

The ABC Model involves simplifying your daily activities into three emotional zones:

A activities: These are the irritating activities you dread. It pains you to do them.

B activities: These activities are just okay. They don't excite you. You don't particularly look forward to doing them. But they're not irritating. Often, they're activities that used to be exciting in the past and now give you a guaranteed result, but just aren't exciting anymore—and never will be again.

C activities: These are the activities you find fascinating and motivating. They give you energy rather than use it up. These are the things you want to focus your time on.

The goal is 100% fascinating and motivating.

Your most important goal for the rest of your entrepreneurial career is to have all of your activities be in the Fascinating & Motivating zone, and spend none of your time, attention, or energy in the Irritating or Okay zones.

To do this, first look at the total amount of time you spend working in an average week and determine what percentage of that time you spend in each of the three zones. This is your baseline measurement. Now, having done this initial inventory, you're ready to improve it.

When people first come into The Strategic Coach Program, it's not unusual for them to be spending 70 percent of their time doing Irritating activities, 25 percent of their time in the Okay zone, and only five percent in the area of Fascinating & Motivating.

Eliminate everything you find irritating.

When you use this ABC tool, your Irritating activities actually become your greatest resource, and the time you spend in the Irritating zone becomes your biggest opportunity for rapid growth. Eliminate those activities and move that time into your Fascinating & Motivating zone, and you'll experience a dramatic improvement in your productivity and enjoyment at work.

A lot of Irritating activities only exist because of unconscious habit. Maybe they were necessary at one stage of your company's development, but now, perhaps *nobody* should be doing them—certainly not you. And if you can't eliminate them entirely, you can at least outsource them to someone else.

The goal with your Irritating activities is to remove them from your time, one way or another, 100 percent. You can do this gradually, just eliminating one or two each quarter.

Delegate/automate everything that's just okay.
Okay activities are crucial for the ongoing success of your company. They're usually connected to your predictable cash flow.

While you won't want to eliminate these activities entirely, you don't have to be the one doing them. There are two ways to free yourself from them. The first is delegation, which involves handing over the activity to someone who, because of their particular skills and interests, would find that task fascinating and motivating. By doing this, you're not only freeing yourself up from something you don't find exciting anymore, you're giving it to someone who will—and who may even be better at it than you were.

The second way is through automation, which is really delegating to a machine. There could be software that can handle the task or machinery that achieves the same result in a fraction of the time.

Ultimately, whether you delegate the activity or automate it, the most important thing is to remove your time from it.

Focus on breakthroughs that require courage.

Many entrepreneurs' greatest career goal is to reach a point where they no longer need courage. Becoming an entrepreneur in itself requires courage in the early years, but many entrepreneurs I've met simply aim to get to a point where everything is convenient, comfortable, and secure. All that risk-taking, initiating new things, being put in positions where they have to start at the bottom of the learning curve—they don't want any of that.

These entrepreneurs tend to get bored with their company after achieving the first level of success because they're not getting rewarded with the experience of courage anymore. They don't feel the same intensity and energy they once did.

Really great entrepreneurs, on the other hand, are always taking on bigger risks, always jumping up to another level. They're as scared at the beginning of their fifth jump as they were at the beginning of the first. They know that moving all of their time into their area of Fascinating & Motivating activities takes a series of committed and courageous improvements.

The Self-Managing Company is not a goal. It's a means. The goal is to become a bigger, better version of yourself by never staying complacent with your time, activities, or goals, and always staying fascinated and motivated.

ELIMINATE ALL IRRITATING

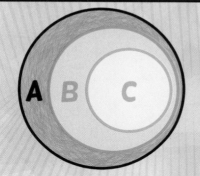

EVERY QUARTER, YOU ELIMINATE ACTIVITIES THAT *IRRITATE* YOU.

DELEGATE/AUTOMATE OKAY

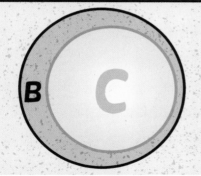

EVERY QUARTER, YOU DELEGATE OR AUTOMATE ACTIVITIES THAT ARE *JUST OKAY*.

100% FASCINATING AND MOTIVATING

EVERY QUARTER, EVERYTHING YOU DO IS INCREASINGLY *FASCINATING AND MOTIVATING*.

Chapter 2
The 4 C's Formula
You increasingly create each new breakthrough on the basis of Commitment, Courage, Capability, and Confidence.

With each shift you make using the ABC Model to move your time and attention out of the areas of Irritating and Okay and into your area of Fascinating and Motivating, a higher level of commitment and a period of courage are required.

Many people feel that before making the commitment to make a significant change, they first need the capability and confidence to do so. I've found, however, that all break-throughs in life happen when a commitment is made first as part of a four-stage process.

Four steps to guaranteed breakthroughs.
The 4 C's Formula involves four important steps to achiev-ing big goals: Commitment, Courage, Capability, and Confidence.

Any significant change in life requires first making a com-mitment to a bigger goal than you've achieved before. This commitment gives structure to the change by defining a measurable result and putting a deadline on it.

When you're making a commitment to change, at first you don't have the capability to do it. But new capabilities get created by making a higher-level commitment and having greater courage when you don't yet know how you're going to pull it off.

The commitment and courage are actually the raw materials

for creating a higher level of capability. The payoff when you achieve the capability is that you get a higher level of confidence—and then you can start the cycle over for another new and exciting goal. Indeed, the best entrepreneurial life lived is one where at any time, you're in one of these 4 C's stages.

Start everything with commitment.

A measurable result and a deadline are the two ingredients that differentiate a commitment from simply being a wish. You might wish that you could spend more of your time doing fascinating and motivating activities, but without specific measurements, it's unlikely to happen.

When you put a number to your goal (e.g., "Spend 80% of my time in Fascinating & Motivating activities") or measure the achievement of your goal by the occurrence of a clear-cut event (e.g., "By next month, I'll no longer be doing any Irritating activities"), you change it from being merely a hope to being a commitment you can actually achieve.

Your higher commitment creates courage.

A lot of people have a hard time making a commitment to a goal without a guarantee that they're going to be successful. The nature of the entrepreneur, however, is that they do it anyway and go through an uncomfortable period of courage, recognizing that it's a necessary stage to reach their goal.

It's a lot easier to be courageous if you have an idea of how long that period of courage will last and what the payoff will be. When you have tangible measurements and deadlines, your period of courage doesn't have to be long at all.

Your commitment to a goal defines your starting point and the reward. When you have that, it helps you to be courageous for a period of time even before you start seeing rewards. You can never get used to courage, but you can get used to having a four-stage process where courage is one of the stages.

For entrepreneurs, it helps to have your team members as witnesses to your commitments as they can keep you accountable to them. Seeing your commitments and the improvements you're making also generates an enormous amount of energy for the team and inspires them to make their own commitments to big goals and to become more self-managing.

Courage triggers new, bigger capability.
It's only once you make a commitment and forge ahead through the discomfort of courage that you discover the means of achieving your goal. Whether it's through teamwork, technology, or a new innovation, the new capability reveals itself.

This new capability would have never appeared if you hadn't first made the commitment and were willing to step into it without knowing how it was going to be done. This willingness to go through a period of courage triggers in your mind an energizing ingenuity and creativity that produces the new, bigger capability that makes the breakthrough possible.

Higher confidence motivates you.
Once you've achieved this new capability and have been able to reach your goal, you gain a new level of confidence.

At this higher level of confidence, you experience things more intensely, your perspective expands, and there's an emotional payoff. But you can't stay in this elevated space forever. After a while, it loses its value.

To be continually growing, it's necessary to keep creating new confidence, and to do that, you have to create new commitments, courage, and capability. With higher confidence, things that were previously uncertain become certain. Things that were previously unclear become clear. Things that were more complex become simpler.

To have a Self-Managing Company, you're not the only person who's going to have to step into new areas. Your commitment and courage in creating greater capabilities and higher confidence puts positive pressure on your team members to do the same thing.

And as more people in your organization use The 4 C's Formula, they'll be in a better position to grow in your Self-Managing Company and free you up to focus only on what fascinates and motivates you.

When you build a Self-Managing Company, you're getting out of the way of certain activities, requiring others on your team to step up and take risks and be fully committed. Having everyone on your team adopt the 4 C's model as their growth process supports them in developing new capabilities and raising their own confidence levels.

But you have to set the example. Growth will be your highest form of leadership.

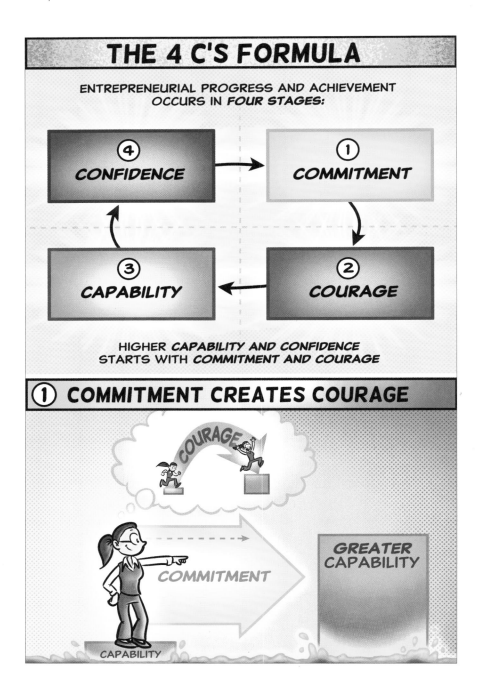

THE 4 C'S FORMULA

ENTREPRENEURIAL PROGRESS AND ACHIEVEMENT
OCCURS IN *FOUR STAGES:*

④ CONFIDENCE

① COMMITMENT

③ CAPABILITY

② COURAGE

HIGHER *CAPABILITY AND CONFIDENCE*
STARTS WITH *COMMITMENT AND COURAGE*

① COMMITMENT CREATES COURAGE

COURAGE

COMMITMENT

CAPABILITY

GREATER CAPABILITY

Chapter 3
The Gap And The Gain

You're always establishing bigger goals ahead of you while measuring your progress backward from where you started.

The entrepreneurial dream of increased freedom exists only in the realm of the ideal until real measurements and deadlines are given to it. Only then does it become an achievable goal.

But, too often, people use the ideal as a measuring stick for their progress, leading only to disappointment and unhappiness.

The ideal only illuminates your goals.

The ideal is like the sun that illuminates the path ahead of you to give you the encouragement to take the necessary steps to reach your destination. Our ideals give us an image in our minds of where we want to go. The purpose of the ideal, however, is not to achieve it, but to use it to throw light on your achievable and measurable goals.

So much unhappiness is experienced in the entrepreneurial world due to a misunderstanding of the difference between ideals and goals. Many entrepreneurs are driven forward incessantly by a growing frustration of not achieving their ideals. But ideals are as achievable as reaching the horizon.

The horizon is a concept that helps your brain to see ahead of you and gauge distance. In the same way, the ideal gives you a sense of what you're aiming for while remaining technically unreachable itself. It's a useful tool, but getting there is impossible.

How you measure is either good or bad.

An ideal can't be measured. It's an anticipated future emotional experience. You believe that when you achieve this particular experience, you're going to feel totally different than you feel right now. But the ideal cannot be reached.

A goal, on the other hand, is a commitment that has measurement and a deadline to it. When you've reached it, you know it.

There are two ways to measure your progress toward your goals:

1. By looking ahead from where you currently are toward your ideal and focusing on how far you have left to go.

2. By looking back from where you currently are to where you started and seeing how far you've come.

The first way leads to unhappiness; the second to happiness.

Measuring against the ideal = unhappiness.

If you're an ideal-measuring person, you're guaranteed to be unhappy. You'll always be comparing your achievements against the ideal, and you'll never measure up. The failure to reach that desired future state erases your sense of your achievements.

Even though from an outside perspective, it looks like you've done remarkable things, you don't feel a sense of accomplishment. When you measure against the ideal, no matter how great your progress is, it always makes you unhappy because you feel like you've failed. You see only the ideal still in the distance.

We call that permanent distance between your actual achievements and your ideal, "The Gap." There's always a gap between what you hope to achieve and what you actually can achieve, and focusing on this gap leads to disappointment and frustration.

Not only are you left feeling a sense of failure, it's impossible to have a Self-Managing Company if you're always in The Gap—if you don't reward yourself as the entrepreneur for your own progress, it becomes impossible for you to reward your team members for their progress. If progress doesn't make you happy, it won't make anyone in your organization happy.

Measuring against the start = happiness.

The other way of measuring your progress is to use the ideal only to illuminate an achievable, measurable goal. But when you get to the goal, instead of looking forward to the ideal, turn around and look back at where you started.

Seeing how far you've come raises your confidence and, as a result, emboldens you to make a commitment to an even bigger future goal. Looking at things this way rewards you and we call this, "The Gain."

Every time you use your starting point to measure your progress, even if it's only modest so far, the feeling of achievement you get leads to happiness.

Record your three wins every day.

A practical step you can take on a daily basis to keep yourself out of The Gap is to measure your progress against your starting point and focus on your achievements. The greatest morale builder, the thing that gives you the greatest sense of momentum, is knowing you've made measurable progress every single day and feeling rewarded by your progress.

Establish a habit of ending each day by looking back at your day and identifying three achievements—or "wins" as we call them. Once you get in the habit of looking for them, you expand your understanding of what can be a win: It could be a really terrific ten-minute meeting that establishes great clarity, it could be completing a project, it could be exercising, it could be spending time with your spouse, and so on.

When you take the time daily to recognize your achievements, you're building a muscle. You can continually train yourself to look for progress, measure progress, and celebrate progress.

Remember that it's your assessment of your situation, not the reality of it, that determines your happiness. It's all about how you look at it and how you measure. Even on your worst day, you can likely find three "wins."

If you want to keep making progress and keep feeling confident enough to make new commitments and go through periods of courage, make sure to keep reinforcing our gains.

Strategic Coach offers a free app called WinStreak, available through the App Store and Google Play, that helps you keep track of your wins on a daily basis and continually set new goals. It makes every day a winning day.

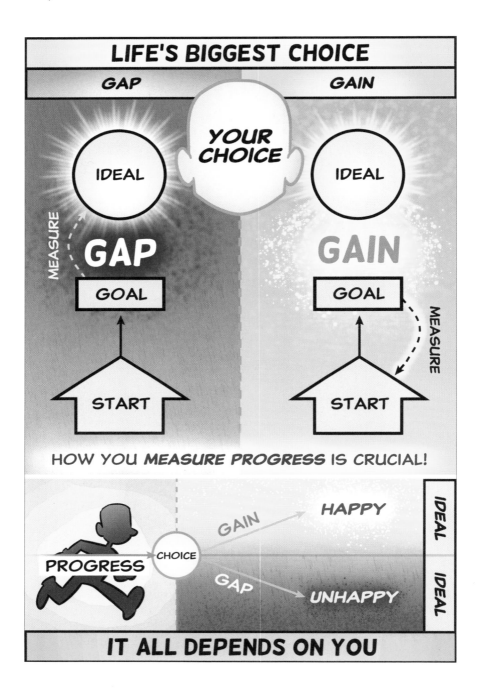

THE GAP = UNHAPPINESS

- *PERFECTIONISM*
- CONTINUAL *DISAPPOINTMENT*
- CHRONIC SENSE OF *FAILURE*
- *BLAMING* OUTSIDE FACTORS
- BEING *PESSIMISTIC*
- BECOMING *CYNICAL* AND *BORED*
- *LOSS* OF *AMBITION*

THE GAIN = HAPPINESS

- GROWING *ACHIEVEMENT*
- *EXCITEMENT*
- *SATISFACTION*
- INCREASING *MOTIVATION*
- GREATER *CONFIDENCE*
- EXPANDING *SUCCESS*
- *OPTIMISM* AND *AMBITION*

YOUR DAILY "WINSTREAK" PROCESS

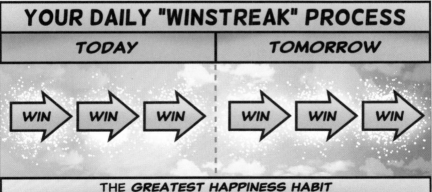

TODAY	TOMORROW
WIN WIN WIN	WIN WIN WIN

THE *GREATEST HAPPINESS HABIT*
ENTREPRENEURS CAN *START RIGHT AWAY*

Chapter 4
Free, Focus, And Buffer Days

You continually manage your daily time to increase personal rejuvenation, productivity, and preparation.

Over the past 42 years, I've had the opportunity of coaching extraordinarily successful entrepreneurs who seem to be miraculously productive and creative. What I've noticed is that their relationship with time is very different from that of the majority of other entrepreneurs and non-entrepreneurs.

Though entrepreneurs free themselves from the kind of work that takes place in corporations, a lot of them pick up and maintain the same time mindsets of those working in bureaucratic organizations. They see themselves as the chief executive officer sitting in the corner office, and they conduct their time accordingly, when, in fact, their life more closely resembles that of a successful entertainer or athlete who tends to schedule their time radically differently from those who work in other jobs or fields.

You can break down their time into three different energy states I call Free Days, Focus Days, and Buffer Days. Focus Days are show time or game time. Entertainers, athletes, and great entrepreneurs focus on doing their most import-ant activities for a short period of time and operate at an extraordinary level of skill and resolve that most people can't.

Buffer Days are just for practice, rehearsal, or preparation for these Focus Days. And Free Days are 24-hour periods of no work-related activities, where the purpose is simply rejuvenation.

Expanding your freedom of time.

Expanding your freedom of time is essential to having a Self-Managing Company. The more you're freed up to concentrate totally on what fascinates and motivates you, the more your company can grow.

Most people don't have boundaries in their time system. The majority of entrepreneurs have the attitude that any one of the 365 days in a year can be a workday if there's an opportunity. Their mindsets practically guarantee that work is always going to be favored over anything in their lives— and *everyone* in their lives.

But when you structure your time according to The Entrepreneurial Time System of Free, Focus, and Buffer Days, you have the freedom to make and carry out all your commitments, personal and professional.

This freedom comes to a certain extent from the restriction. If you say that Free Days are work-free days and you stick to it, that frees you up to be free. Likewise, on Focus Days, you're freed up for higher productivity and profitability, and on Buffer Days, you're freed up to have your mind on preparation without worrying about anything else.

It's the greatest freedom to be able to focus on one thing completely without feeling that you should be doing something else.

Free Days for rejuvenation.

The important thing to note about Free Days is that they come first. Unlike in most time systems where vacation days are a reward for hard work, in The Entrepreneurial Time

System, Free Days are booked first and are a prerequisite for top-notch Focus and Buffer Days.

To double your income, you have to double your free time—as counterintuitive as that my seem. Once you've booked off your free time, whatever is left over is the amount of time you have to get your work done, which forces you to be increasingly productive during that time.

Focus Days for productivity.

When I encounter entrepreneurs who can't quite wrap their minds around the idea of Focus Days—24-hour periods where you focus only on your three most important money-making activities—I remind them that throughout their life, they've actually had Focus Days that were determined by deadline commitments where they had only a short amount of time to get a great deal done. They always made their deadlines by putting everything else aside to focus and to perform in an enormously productive and efficient way.

The problem is that most people won't take this focusing time without deadline coercion. They won't do it unless their reputation is at stake. But what if you could do it without the threat and the pressure?

By giving definition to your time and separating out your days, you prevent your activities and responsibilities from getting jumbled up in such a way that different things are always competing for your attention.

When you allow yourself an entire day to stay focused, with no interference from anything else, you notice just how much you can get done.

Buffer Days for preparation.

Too often, entrepreneurs don't take the time to practice or rehearse for their Focus Days. They're like actors who show up on opening night and don't know their lines but expect the audience to be very pleased with the $100 ticket they purchased.

People have different ways of rehearsing, but anybody who's good at anything does an enormous amount of testing things offstage so that during performance time, they don't have to think about it.

You can't perform and test at the same time. Buffer Days are for all the clean-ups, delegations, thinking, and rehearsing—so that during the "performance," you can just be in the moment and at your very best.

Each day supports the other two.

None of the types of days are possible without the other two. Free Days rejuvenate you so that you can be alert and creative on Focus Days and eliminate "stuff" and messes on Buffer Days. Focus Days allow you to get your most important activities done efficiently and productively so that your Buffer Days can be just for preparation and your Free Days can be truly free. Buffer Days give you time to focus on just the clean-ups and preparation that need to be done so you have nothing to worry about on your Free Days and are free from interruptions on Focus Days.

When you keep these days separate and use them as planned, you free yourself up from distractions that take you off course. You also model the Time System for your team so they can become more self-managing.

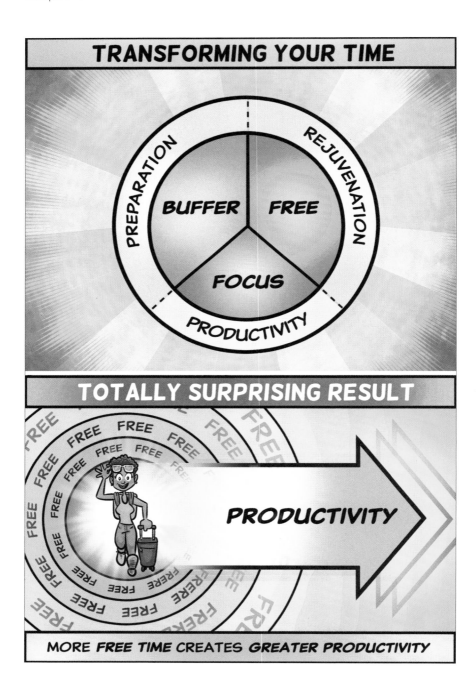

MORE ENERGIZED

REJUVENATION

YOU USE INCREASED FREE TIME TO RE-ENERGIZE EVERY AREA OF YOUR LIFE.

- GREATER *SIMPLICITY*
- GREATER *PERSPECTIVE*
- GREATER *CLARITY*

MORE PROFITABLE

PRODUCTIVITY

YOU MULTIPLY YOUR BEST ABILITIES, RELATIONSHIPS, AND OPPORTUNITIES.

- GREATER *PERFORMANCE*
- GREATER *ACHIEVEMENTS*
- GREATER *RESULTS*

MORE CONFIDENT

PREPARATION

YOU CONTINUALLY ANTICIPATE AND EXPAND YOUR FUTURE-BASED ADVANTAGES.

- GREATER *PLANNING*
- GREATER *TEAMWORK*
- GREATER *TECHNOLOGY*

Chapter 5
Unique Ability Teamwork

You continually simplify and multiply your own contribution by expanding your teamwork with uniquely talented individuals in every area of life.

While most people work within structures they didn't organize themselves, entrepreneurs get to organize their systems from scratch.

They act as role models for everyone who comes to work at their company, which means that if they're spending time on things they're not good at, then everyone working for them will follow suit.

But teams work best when each person is focused only on activities they love and do best—their Unique Ability.

Having a Unique Ability Team means working out a deal whereby each person is freed up to focus on their own area of Unique Ability. It means hiring people with diverse skills and talents, including in areas where you're lacking, so that each task and responsibility in your business is covered by someone who loves doing it and is best at it.

Your team members will only work this way, though, once they've gotten permission to do that from your example. They can't give themselves any more permission than you demonstrate.

Always fascinating and motivating.

Every time you achieve a new breakthrough that increases the amount of time, attention, and energy you spend in activities that fascinate and motivate you, the more you're operating in your Unique Ability.

Unique Ability requires you to determine what you person-ally like and dislike doing, and decide that others' opinions about it are irrelevant. The basis of Unique Ability is to con-tinually be conscious of the activities and the settings you like and that energize you—and the things that don't.

This is where freedom starts: with the understanding that your own judgments about your own experience are 100 percent valid.

Passion, hero, and multipliers.

Your Unique Ability is composed of those specific skills you're passionate about doing. If you were to spend ten hours doing it in a very concentrated way, you'd be gener-ating more energy than you'd be using up. You wouldn't be tired; you'd be excited.

When you use these skills you're passionate about to help another person, that person will see you as a hero. Heroism doesn't have to involve sacrificing yourself; it can just involve being at the service of someone else in a way that nothing else could be.

Focus this passionate heroism on those entrepreneurial situ-ations that lead to the continual multiplication of your results and rewards. This is what Unique Ability is all about.

Unique Ability leadership by example.

Your most important leadership activity in developing and expanding a Self-Managing Company lies in continually moving all of your time into just those activities that are in your area of Unique Ability.

This demonstrates what everyone else in your company needs to do to become self-managing.

The more you give yourself permission to spend time doing certain things and not others, the more you give others the permission to do this too.

There's no end to the number of people you can inspire with this vision, because there's a natural incentive in people to operate this way. They'd like to make a difference, they'd like to be energized, and they'd like to see the multiplication of their results on a continual basis.

We spend a third of our lifetime working. We might as well make sure that this time is not spent doing activities that are draining or exhausting, for ourselves or for those working for us. We want the work and the teamwork to be energizing.

All of that needs to start with you, as the entrepreneur, giving yourself permission to be that way, and then others will choose whether they want to be part of that. Gradually, you start attracting the right team members, and teamwork grows among people who really want to be in your organization.

True for you, true for everyone.
Every time you free yourself up more to operate in your Unique Ability, the more possible it becomes for every member of your team to do the same.

You can never grant any freedom to yourself that you're not willing to grant to someone else. All of life is a teamwork experience.

Just as it's true that your team won't feel they have permission to free themselves up to focus on their areas of Unique Ability without your leadership example, it's also the case that you won't be able to focus on your Unique Ability and achieve a Self-Managing Company unless your team members are also freed up to focus on what they love to do and do best—those things that give them energy, and therefore, energize the entire organization.

Teamwork that expands itself.

Unlike in the environments of typical large corporations, there are no "superior" or "inferior" skills when you're operating within the Unique Ability concept. The only distinction is uniqueness. In bureaucratic organizations, some people are free and others aren't; some people get rewarded and others don't.

But in an entrepreneurial company, everyone is freed up, and the more you can operate from this Unique Ability foundation, the more you can take advantage of new technologies and opportunities in the world.

To give this kind of freedom to your team requires a profound shift in your thinking, but you'll increasingly enjoy greater creative and collaborative support for your own Unique Ability as more of your team members are able to focus entirely on theirs.

My presence isn't required for my team to do their best work, and this continual development and expansion of everyone's Unique Ability Teamwork automatically creates a Self-Managing Company.

FASCINATING AND MOTIVATING

- PASSION
- HERO
- MULTIPLIERS

THREE UNIQUE ABILITY EXPANDERS

① PASSION

THE ACTIVITY GENERATES *MORE ENERGY* THAN IT USES.

② HERO

YOUR ACTIVITY CREATES NEW VALUE THAT *TRANSFORMS* OTHERS' LIVES.

PAF!

③ MULTIPLIERS

THE ACTIVITY CONTINUALLY *ACCELERATES* YOUR PROGRESS AND RESULTS.

Chapter 6

The Largest Check

You continually achieve bigger and more profitable sales that increase your capabilities and confidence for even bigger sales.

Shifting your mindsets regarding teamwork and how you're scheduling your time has huge results, but the proof that you're really doing something better is in the size of the checks your company receives.

As your company becomes more self-managing and you and your team are able to focus more and more on your own areas of Unique Ability, you'll be able to achieve increasingly bigger financial results—as long as you, as the entrepreneur, have the mindset of always increasing the size of your "Largest Check."

Your Current Largest Check.

By "check," I mean the total amount of money you've received from a client or customer in a single year. This money may come to you in one lump-sum payment or in a series of smaller payments. You can determine your Current Largest Check by identifying the five largest amounts you've received in the last 12 months and calculating the average.

In my own experience, when I came up with my first break-through concept and began coaching it one on one, I made $20,000 in the first year. Half of that came from my top five clients, so my Largest Check back then was $2,000.

Then I hit a ceiling where I knew I'd never get above my current size of check unless I changed the game. This led to my switching to coaching workshops rather than coaching one on one, simultaneously creating more value for my clients while increasing the amount I could get paid for the same amount of time invested.

Entrepreneurial building blocks.

This created a huge jump in revenue, and yet the work became incredibly more enjoyable and I could focus more and more on solving my clients' biggest issues. Since then, I've taken several more jumps, increasing my Largest Check each time. Between $2,000 as your Largest Check and $1.5 million, for example, as your Largest Check, there are about 25 increasingly bigger checks in the middle. It's like a stairway where every step up is a Largest Check.

Your progress as an entrepreneur has been constructed of ever bigger and better sales, and each time you took a jump in the size of a sale, you also increased your sense of capability and confidence to go even higher. Each time you visualized receiving an even bigger check than what you'd been achieving, it required a higher level of commitment and greater courage.

With each jump, though, you're also increasing the value you provide. After all, you want those people who are paying $1.5 million to feel certain that they're getting the better part of the deal. Indeed, your confidence as an entrepreneur is largely dependent on your having the sense that your client is receiving more value than you are.

Establish your Next Largest Check.

Increasing your performance and achievement starts with creating a baseline of where you are right now. The Largest Check creates a new starting point. Your Current Largest Check is the biggest you've ever achieved, but it becomes your next jumping off point to reaching even higher levels of productivity and profitability.

Consider people who climb Mt. Everest. They stop at camps along the way before reaching the summit, which means they can concentrate their efforts only on the next highest goal. Once they've reached the next camp, what they were striving for becomes the new starting point, and then they move on to the next level.

If they had been anticipating the highest, most difficult peak at the very start, they would have been discouraged along the way. But you're never going for that bigger goal until it's the next one to achieve.

Setting your Minimum Check.

To accelerate your progress in achieving your Next Largest Check, you increasingly move your time and attention out of areas of Irritating and Okay activities and into those that are Fascinating and Motivating—in other words, into Unique Ability. And your team will be doing the same thing.

This means that many smaller sales and checks that were Okay in the past are now becoming Irritating to your entire organization. To bring your company's check-getting capabilities up to date and focused on a bigger future, it's important to establish a Minimum Check. Your Minimum Check dictates that you, as the entrepreneur, will no longer be personally involved in sales or client management where the result is less than a specific amount you determine.

As you grow, previous levels you've achieved no longer contribute to the productivity or profitability of your organization, and certain clients are more of a drain on your company than a benefit to it, especially if you're the one handling those clients yourself.

There are two strategies for dealing with this. You can eliminate the clients who are taking up your time but not giving you the results of your Largest Check clients by referring them to other organizations. Or you can hand over those clients to your team members as a means of training them and helping them grow, improving your team's self-managing capabilities by giving them this added responsibility. In either case, you, yourself, are freed up to focus on your top results-producing clients.

Visualizing your Dream Check.

You know from your entrepreneurial career so far that much of what keeps you fascinated, motivated, and passionate about your future comes from dreaming about a huge sale that's exponentially larger than anything you've achieved in the past. This big future goal is your Dream Check.

Right now, you might not yet have the capabilities or confidence to get to this result, but you're increasingly mastering the mindsets and skills that are developing and expanding your Self-Managing Company, which means that in the future, this Dream Check will become your Next Largest Check and then your Current Largest Check.

Entrepreneurs are perpetually aware that there are always bigger goals to achieve, and there is always a larger check that you have in mind. Your Dream Check is what keeps you continually striving, improving, and growing, never satisfied with the status quo and always looking to up your game.

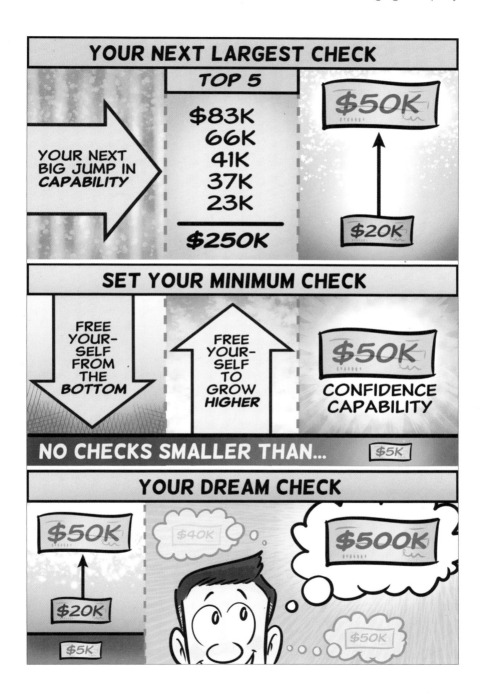

Chapter 7
The 10x Mind Expander
You're continually creating greater opportunities and capabilities to achieve 10x greater income and profits by a specific deadline.

It's been my experience from 42 years of coaching that you can have every other mindset we've discussed so far in this book and still might not produce the Self-Managing Company you find satisfying. This is because you may be in a market or a setting where you can continually improve and grow—but only incrementally.

There isn't enough "energetic confidence" about the future to catalyze everybody in your company to free you up completely to just focus on growth unless you have what most people would call an outrageous goal. 10x is one of those ideas that in a very short period will stretch your brain in such a way that it can't go back to its previous form.

To expand your mind in this way, start by taking your last year's total revenues and multiplying it by ten in your mind. We're going to use that number as a thinking tool for making changes in the present. The moment you do this, the new 10x goal will encourage and motivate you and your team to become even more of a Self-Managing Company.

You've already achieved 10x growth.
Entrepreneurs, for the most part, don't look backward, but it can be a great way to build your confidence for the future.

Take your previous year's best income result and look back to a time when you were achieving only one-tenth of that. Now, look forward from then to today and the results you're getting right now. Did you know then how you would get to where you are today? Probably not. It required a lot of commitment and courage and an increase in capability and confidence.

But you did it. You might have even gone 10x in your business more than once so far, and each time, you didn't know how you would pull it off.

Looking forward now to another 10x jump, you can see that the process will be similar, only now you'll be achieving much faster progress because you and your team will be operating entirely within the mindsets of a Self-Managing Company.

Growing 10x is easier than going 2x.

It's important to note that aiming for a 10x transformation is superior in every way to merely doubling your current results.

If you're only thinking about taking your present income and profits 2x, no one in your company, including you, is going to be excited about the goal, the process, or the outcome.

You can probably accomplish it over time without any radical examination of how everyone is operating right now. With a 2x goal, your team will see that not much change on their part is needed to actually pull it off.

An "outrageous" goal like 10x, on the other hand, requires an entirely different kind of game. You know you can't work 10x longer or 10x harder. You can't continually increase quantity and create a different kind of quality.

With a 10x goal, you have to take your future progress out of the realm of time and effort. You're forced to find a new way of getting these major results—which in fact will take far less time and effort and will only be possible with a Self-Managing Company.

Giving yourself 25 years to do it.

I often say, there are no unreasonable goals, only unreasonable deadlines. When people are first presented with the prospect of multiplying 10x, they find it scary because it seems impossible. But it only seems impossible because the moment you said you're going to go 10x, you also applied a deadline to it. And it's not the goal that's scaring you; it's the deadline.

But what if you gave yourself 25 years to go 10x? Does it still seem like an impossible goal? Or would 25 years actually be more than enough time to achieve that goal? Could you go 10x in 15 years? That would give you 10 years left over.

All of a sudden, the idea that you can't go 10x because you don't have enough time immediately switches to, "I can easily go 10x because I have more than enough time."

It's this mindset shift that makes it a very real and attainable goal, not only for you, but also for your team. Asking your team members to work 10x longer and 10x harder isn't going to go over well. But when you tell them that you're giving this goal 25 years, it gives them breathing room as well, and lets them know that it's going to require Unique Ability Teamwork and a constant move into their areas of Fascinating and Motivating activities.

Crucial importance of the 10x deadline.

Most people would have no need to think 25 years ahead because they'd never need 25 years to do anything they're doing today. But if you're achieving an "unreasonable goal," you have to create a deadline that makes that unreasonable goal not only reasonable, but easy.

Think of yourself and your company at the beginning of a 25-year growth curve with today's date at the bottom of the curve and the calendar date that is exactly 25 years from today at the top. Now, going up the curve, put a dot on the line that represents your first estimate of when you and your team will achieve your 10x greater income goal.

This dot is your working deadline right now, and the moment you know what it is, your brain will immediately go into action to discover entirely new ways of reaching that goal in the fastest, easiest, and least costly manner.

Self-managing as fast as possible.

Taking your business 10x is only possible by ensuring that you and everyone on your team is operating as quickly as possible within a Self-Managing Company.

The first time you grew 10x, you didn't have any of the self-managing mindsets you're now mastering. And every one of these mindsets will also make total sense to everyone on your team.

The faster you include everyone in your self-managing and 10x vision, the faster they'll move out of Irritating and Okay activities and into their specific areas of Fascinating and Motivating and their Unique Ability, where they can truly grow—and grow your company as well.

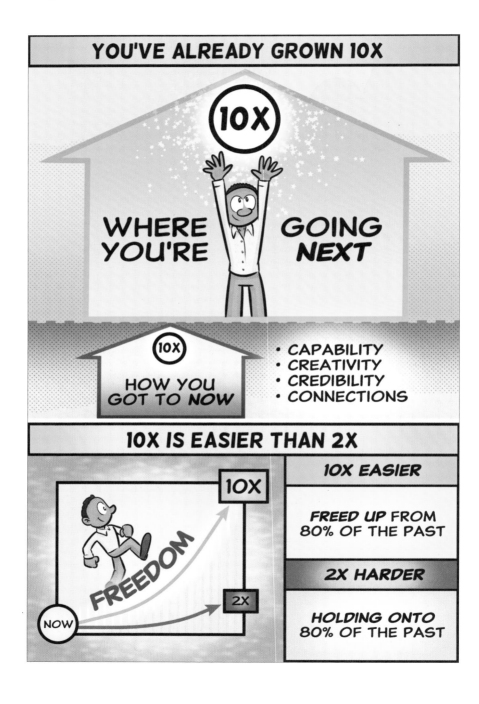

Chapter 8
The Lifetime Extender
You continually expand your motivation to work and live energetically, far beyond conventional expectations and averages.

All of the Self-Managing Company mindsets I've covered in the first seven chapters of this book put you in a position to create and enjoy a uniquely extraordinary lifetime.

But there is a fixed mindset that many people have about how long their lifetime will be. This mindset comes from certain types of statistics that are commonly bantered about, but those types of statistics are geared toward everybody; they don't take into account people who give exceptional performance.

A long time ago, I decided that I wanted to take advantage of the improvements being created as a result of breakthroughs in society in order to see how long I could live. I'm lucky in terms of my physical make-up and my upbringing, and luck is half of the story. I felt that I could put an age out in front of me that was far beyond the conventional human lifespan and work toward that.

My plan for living to 156.
A lot of how you act as an individual has an enormous amount to do with certain kinds of expectations you have for yourself. Many people die at eighty because they expected to die at eighty; having that age in mind as a life expectancy directed how they took care of themselves. I've noticed that about 20 years before the age at which they expect to die, people start arranging their lives so that dying at that age becomes a self-fulfilling prophecy.

I decided to put a fantastical number out there and see how my brain responded to it. I came up with 156 because I wanted the experience of living a complete calendar century, and I was born in 1944. Now, at an age when most people are shutting down, I'm getting bigger because I made the entrepreneurial decision to choose the number that would dictate my behavior.

If you have a goal to live to an extraordinary age, it will have a daily impact on how you take care of yourself presently. The lesson from my goal of living to 156 isn't about making it to the specific age of 156, but rather the ongoing impact that the goal of living to 156 has on my energetic confidence as a creative entrepreneur right now.

Tell yourself how long you'll live.

My number-one formula in life is that your eyes only see and your ears only hear what your brain is looking for. Once I decided to choose the age I'd live to, I suddenly started picking up on information from the frontiers of longevity science, life extension science, and life extension technology. I became aware that if you look in the right places, you'll see that enormous things are happening to support living longer.

If you don't tell yourself how long you'll live, other people will tell you. If you decide on a specific year when you intend to die, and you recognize that this future date is continually adjustable as you move toward it, you instantly make your entire life intentional.

This also means that you take complete responsibility for everything that's happened and everything that will happen, from your birth to your death.

Friends, money, and purpose.

The vast majority of people are increasing their likelihood of dying sooner than necessary because as they age, they're losing their friends, they're running out of money, and they no longer have a compelling purpose to stay alive.

People tend to be friends with those their own age, and this can have a strong influence on you if you perceive that the people closest to you are dying off. The body responds to loneliness and to the perception that you don't have anyone with whom to share your experience of going forward.

A solution to avoid this is to continually increase the number of friends you have who are younger than you are, keeping in mind that you can take anyone of any age seriously as an individual because of their Unique Ability and what they uniquely bring to the table, regardless of their age.

As you get old, you may also run out of money, making you dependent, which may make you feel like a burden to others. You'll feel like you're leading an increasingly useless existence in relation to other people, and this feeling may encourage you to die earlier than you otherwise would. Understanding this idea now will give you the motivation to maintain financial independence as you get older.

The final encouragement to death is the lack of a purpose. You don't want to feel like there's nothing ahead of you that will be bigger than what you've already been through. It's vital to have a compelling purpose to stay alive. Having a purpose and always envisioning a bigger future, no matter what your age, is what keeps you always looking forward to the future.

The mindset x technology formula.

At any given time, you're either working in a useful, growing partnership with the world or you're not, and this affects your mindset about what's possible in the future. There's a collective capability that's growing in the world, and it makes it increasingly useful for focused people to get ahead faster than ever before.

How long you live will increasingly be a function of your longevity mindsets multiplied by emerging life extension science and technology.

As an entrepreneur who's always expanding your freedom of time, money, relationship, and purpose, you're in an increasingly favorable position to take advantage of the latest cutting-edge breakthroughs in extending the healthiest possible human longevity during the 21st century.

Self-Managing Company advantage.

As you live your ever-expanding life and continually enjoy the greater protection and support of your growing Self-Managing Company, your unique entrepreneurial organization will constantly be freeing you up even more to focus all of your greater commitment, courage, capability, and confidence on only those activities that fascinate and motivate you.

And with that experience, who wouldn't want to live to 156?

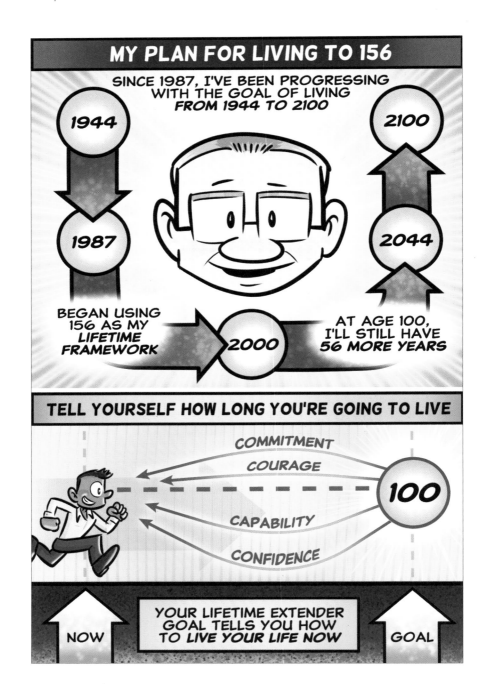

Conclusion
Getting Ready To Self-Multiply
You continually master the eight self-managing mindsets in order to build your Self-Multiplying Company.

Each of the mindsets in The Self-Managing Company acts as a filter that distinguishes those activities that grow your energy from those that drain it. As you move forward on this extraordinary entrepreneurial path, you'll see that this new organizational capability is a platform that will enable you to jump to an even higher level of growth.

This is where everything in your company is not only self-managing but begins to be self-multiplying in ways that position you as a permanent Game Changer force in your industry and market.

The Self-Managing Company isn't the end goal; it's the preparation for something entirely new. While some people might see a Self-Managing Company as enabling them to no longer have to work and to just make money on auto-pilot, there are others who see that everything they've done so far was to get to the point where they could really play the big game.

Freed up to grow exponentially.
The really big game is being a full participant in the current economic, technological, and scientific world that provides the ability to multiply your results. When you build a self-managing team around you, you set up the conditions for everyone to take initiative and volunteer their unique skills and innovations in order to make improvements you might never have considered otherwise.

When a new situation arises that requires ingenuity, your self-managing team members are in a position to take responsibility and come up with solutions using their Unique Ability. With a Self-Managing Company, you're able to multiply your impact in response to the circumstances, and exponential, rather than incremental, growth becomes a real possibility.

By continually strengthening, developing, and expanding your Self-Managing Company, you take maximum advantage of the exponential multipliers the world is creating.

Being self-managing keeps you uniquely simple.
The greatest advantage of having a Self-Managing Company is that you and your team are always experiencing greater simplicity, clarity, and confidence while your competitors are experiencing increasing complexity, confusion, and uncertainty.

As one of our clients pointed out in his workshop, the overall focus of The Strategic Coach Program can be simplified down to helping people increasingly do the right things with the right people and spend less time doing the wrong things with the wrong people.

Unique Ability Teamwork lays the groundwork for simplifying your role in your company. I know that there are three things I'm really good at: coaching, coming up with new ideas, and the packaging and marketing of those ideas. Outside of that, vast other skills and abilities exist in the company to take on every other task. The simplicity of this means I can focus on what I do best without worrying about anything else.

Partnering with the best technology.

Your growing Self-Managing Company based on expanding Unique Ability Teamwork is increasingly in the best possible position to take advantage of new technological tools, systems, and networks.

One of the great fallacies about technology is that it's something outside of ourselves. But technology always starts with teamwork that becomes so predictable and reliable, you can automate it. Technology is just automated teamwork. In the same way you can partner up with a team member, you can also partner with technology. Technology actually grows most in its usefulness to human teamwork. If you want to know where the best technologies are developing on the planet, it's in the places that most lend themselves to partnering with existing top-notch teamwork.

Never fatigued and never bored.

The Self-Managing Company protects you from being fatigued or bored. In my experience as an entrepreneur, the fatigue and boredom factor at age seventy-two is a fraction of what it was 30 years ago. I can tell when I go on Free Days that I'm not tired anymore. In the evenings, I'm not tired anymore. I used to take naps during the day, but I don't anymore because there isn't anything I'm doing right now that drains my energy.

There are no longer things that annoy me. There are no people around who annoy me. I never get bored because everything we're taking on lies in the area of the new and fascinating. I still go through The 4 C's Formula and make commitments to big goals that scare me and require a period of courage. This is what leads to new capabilities and confidence, which in turn leads me to make even bigger commitments and take on new challenges. Boredom can never make its way in when you're continually challenging yourself to reach new levels of success.

A lot of people want to get to a point where they don't have to go through the emotional uncertainty of wondering whether they can pull off another breakthrough. But it's that willingness to go through periods of courage that keeps you endlessly fascinated and motivated.

Being a Game Changer for everyone.

Everyone who keeps maximizing their responsibility is automatically a game changer in any setting where other people aren't taking responsibility. Those who take 100 percent responsibility are the ones who create their own reality, and the others are just waiting for someone else to create it for them. A game changer comes from a profound shift in the source of energy. In any situation, the most intentional person always gets what they want, and everybody else has to go along.

When you're a game changer, you're a net gain to the world around you. You're continually contributing more to every situation you're in than you're taking out. Most people want to see how much they can get with the least amount of contribution.

You're increasingly operating as an inspiring role model to a growing number of other successful entrepreneurs, and your Self-Managing Company becomes the game-changing model that every other successful company learns from, imitates, and follows.

The Strategic Coach Program
Expanding Entrepreneurial Freedom

The Strategic Coach Program, launched in 1989, has qualifications, measurements, structures, and processes that attract a particular type of talented, successful, and ambitious entrepreneur.

One differentiating quality of these Strategic Coach participants is that they recognize that the technology-empowered 21st century is a unique time to be an entrepreneur. It's the first time that a growing number of individuals with no special birth privileges and no special education can achieve almost anything they set their minds to.

These self-motivated individuals who participate in the three levels of Strategic Coach accept that if they can focus on mastering the right mindsets, they can experience increasing breakthroughs for themselves, both personally and professionally, that are new in history.

The Self-Managing Company is one of these breakthrough mindsets, and there are dozens more for you to master.

Mindsets that enable entrepreneurs to escape.
Many entrepreneurs have the potential and the willingness to achieve exponential goals in the 21st century, but they are blocked from taking action and making progress because they feel trapped in three ways:

• **Trapped thinking:** They are isolated by their own disconnected creativity, which continually churns out ideas that don't translate into achievement. *At Strategic Coach, entrepreneurs increasingly liberate their thinking to create entirely new practical breakthroughs for themselves and others.*

• **Trapped circumstances:** They are surrounded by people who don't support their ambitions, who actively oppose them, or who try to make them feel guilty about their achievements and dreams. *At Strategic Coach, entrepreneurs learn how to increasingly surround themselves with like-minded and like-motivated individuals in every area of their personal and business lives.*

• **Trapped energy:** They're using much of their daily energy to simply sustain themselves without ever actually experiencing exponential performance and results. They wanted to create a growing business but it turns out that they've only created a job—one that always stays the same. *At Strategic Coach, entrepreneurs continually transform every part of their business organizations so that they become self-managing, and then self-multiplying.*

Mindsets that enable entrepreneurs to achieve.

Around the world, the vast majority of entrepreneurs never get out of these trapped circumstances, but at Strategic Coach, our participants not only escape from these limitations, they also jump to extraordinary levels of achievement, success, and satisfaction.

They never stop growing. Strategic Coach participants continually transform how they think, how they make decisions, how they communicate, and how they take action based on their mastery of dozens of unique entrepreneurial mindsets that have been developed in the Program. These are purely entrepreneurial mindsets, like The Self-Managing Company.

We've taken a look at what goes on in the minds of the best

entrepreneurs and have created a thinking system that is custom-designed for them and adjusts to the ambition of each individual.

The Strategic Coach Program provides an accelerating lifetime structure, process, and community for these entrepreneurs to create exponential breakthroughs.

Mindsets that enable entrepreneurs to multiply.
Depending on where you are right now in your life and business, we have a complete set of entrepreneurial mindsets that will immediately jump you up to the next level in terms of your ambition, achievements, and progress. Over the course of your entrepreneurial lifetime, you can move upward through our three levels of mindset measurement and scoring:

1. The Strategic Coach Signature Program: From isolation to teamwork. At this first breakthrough level, you create a Unique Ability Team that allows you to have a Self-Managing Company. Every successful entrepreneur dreams about having this kind of teamwork and this kind of organization. Through the Signature level of the Program, these dreams become a reality. In Strategic Coach, the Self-Managing Company is a practical growth system, not a motivational slogan.

2. The 10x Ambition Program: From teamwork to exponential. You make breakthroughs that transform your life, and your organization becomes a Self-Multiplying Company. Talented entrepreneurs want to free their biggest growth plans from non-supportive relationships, situations, and circumstances. Through the 10x Ambition level of Strategic Coach, their biggest aspirations attract multiplier capabilities, resources, and opportunities.

3. The Game Changer Program: From exponential to transformative. As your entrepreneurial life becomes exponential, your Self-Multiplying Company become transformative. *The key evidence of this is that your biggest competitors want to become your best students, customers, and promoters.* Game Changer entrepreneurs in Strategic Coach become the leading innovators and cutting-edge teachers in their industries and continually introduce new strategies, methods, and systems that create *new* industries.

Measure yourself, score yourself, get started.

The back cover of this book folds out into a Mindset Scorecard you can use to score yourself according to the eight mindsets discussed in this book. You can also access a digital copy at *strategiccoach.com/go/SMCEBOOK*. Read through the four statements for each mindset and give yourself a score of 1 to 12 based on where your own mindset falls on the spectrum. Put each mindset's score in the first column at the right, and then add up all eight and put the total at the bottom. Now, think about what scores would represent progress over the next quarter. Write these in the "Next" column, add them up, and write in the total.

When you compare the two scores, you can see where you want to go in terms of your achievements and ambitions. If this fast exercise tells you that you want to multiply in all these areas, contact us today to get started:

The Strategic Coach Program is ready for you! Visit us online at *strategiccoach.com* or call us at 416.531.7399 or 1.800.387.3206.

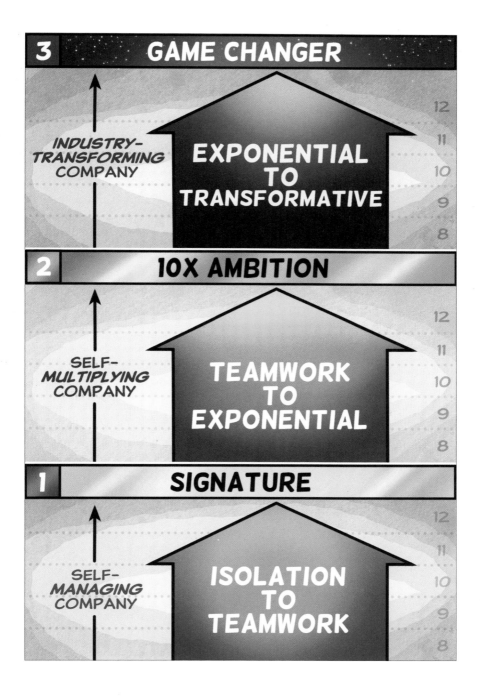

About The Author
Dan Sullivan

 Dan Sullivan is the founder and president of The Strategic Coach Inc. and creator of the Strategic Coach® Program, which helps accomplished entrepreneurs reach new heights of success and happiness. He has over 40 years of experience as a strategic planner and coach to entrepreneurial individuals and groups. He is author of over 30 publications, including *The 80% Approach*™, *The Dan Sullivan Question*, *Ambition Scorecard*, *Wanting What You Want*, *The 4 C's Formula*, *The 25-Year Framework*, *The Game Changer*, *The 10x Mind Expander*, and *The Mindset Scorecard* and is co-author with Catherine Nomura of *The Laws of Lifetime Growth*.